Leo Brouwer

An Idea
for guitar

An Idea was written for the
75th Birthday of Eli Kassner
at Cordoba, April 1999.

Chester Music

AN IDEA

(Passacaglia for Eli)

Leo Brouwer, 1999

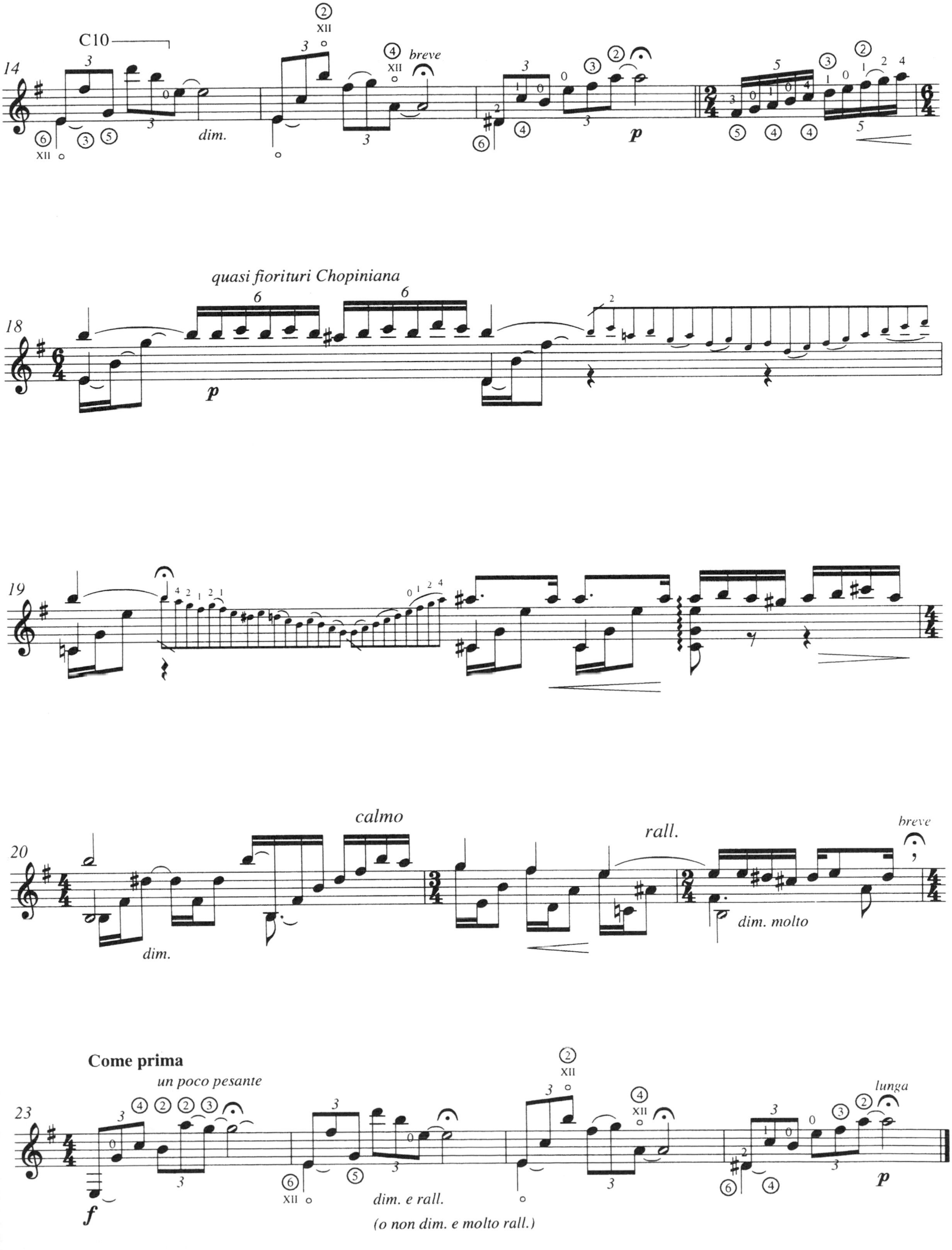
C10
breve
dim.
quasi fiorituri Chopiniana
calmo
dim.
rall.
breve
dim. molto
Come prima
un poco pesante
lunga
dim. e rall.
(o non dim. e molto rall.)